FIND A JOB

The *Little Book*
— FOR —
BIG SUCCESS

To ~
Mark ~
High Value
Activity discipline
works !
Thank you for
teaching me good
stuff.
~ Gaye
Lindfors

FIND A JOB

The *Little Book*
⤝ FOR ⤜
BIG SUCCESS

Gaye Lindfors

ISBN 10: 1-931945-97-7
ISBN 13: 978-1-931945-97-4

Library of Congress Catalog Number: 2009933142

Printed in the United States of America

First Printing: August 2009

12 11 10 09 08   5 4 3 2 1

Andover,
Minnesota

Expert Publishing, Inc.
14314 Thrush Street NW
Andover, MN 55304-3330
1-877-755-4966
www.expertpublishinginc.com

For
My nieces, Kelsey and Julia Charron,
and
My nephews, David, Dan, and Scott Benedict.

Always remember how significant your lives are.
Find the joy in living your definition of big success.
Have fun!

And for Steve. Always.

Table of Contents

Acknowledgements / xi

Introduction / *1*

**A $20 Bill is Still a $20 Bill
After It's Been Through the Wash**
You are Significant / 3

Scream in Your Pillow or Buy a Punching Bag
Work Through Your Emotions / 7

Appoint Yourself CEO
Create a Good Support Team / 13

Play with a Yo-Yo
Prepare a Resume That Makes You Stand Out / 19

**Call Aunt Betty and
Uncle Earl and Cousin Ed and…**
Network, Network, Network / 35

**Wear a Sherlock Holmes Cap
and Grab a Magnifying Glass**
Do Your Research / 47

Take Center Stage and Perform Exceptionally
Ace Your Interview / 53

Watch Miss America or Mr. Universe Pageants
Create a Strategy for Finding Your Next Job / 67

Develop a Simple System for Big Success
Organize Your Job Search Materials / 73

Keep Your Eye on the Ball
Stay Focused on Finding a Job / 81

Go Fishin'
Take Time for Yourself / 85

Significance and Success!
A Note From Gaye / 89

Resources */ 93*

About the Illustrator */ 95*

About the Author */ 97*

Acknowledgements

I love to read. My mom taught me how when I was two years old, and I haven't put a book down since. There's a ritual I follow as I begin turning the pages of a new book. Once I've got my highlighter, pen, notebook, and Diet Pepsi at my side, my attention goes first to the acknowledgements. That's because I want to know something about the author. I want to make a connection with her, catch a glimpse into who and what is important in her life. Feeling like she and I have been introduced helps me better understand the story she's telling, whether it's fiction or non-fiction.

So as I thank the people who have influenced the writing of this book, I'm hoping you and I make a connection. Enjoy this peek into part of my world of significance and success.

My parents taught me that my life is important, and life is worth living. Even though my Dad left this earth a few years ago, I can still hear him enthusiastically pronounce, "This is livin'!" Even in the toughest times, life was good because they trusted in God's faithfulness. And work? It was all about service. Thanks, Mom and Dad, for teaching me how to do what I love and love what I do.

My mentor and friend Laurie Beth Jones (and one of my most favorite authors!) helped me discover my purpose for being on this earth. What a gift! Thank you, Laurie Beth, for helping me make the connection between my purpose, my passion, and my career. Because of you, I know how to define success in my own terms while living my significant life.

Job seekers, especially those who have been laid off, have a special place in my heart. Jane Salmen has given me the delightful opportunity to collaborate with her in providing outplacement services through her company, BluePrint. Thank you for trusting me with your clients, Jane. It is a joy partnering with you.

Audrey Thomas is a friend and National Speakers Association (NSA) colleague. She has held me accountable for taking the time to write this book, and has been my cheerleader and butt-kicker at just the right times. Audrey, thank you for your gift of time and encouragement.

If you're looking for an ideal publishing company to work with, I enthusiastically recommend Harry and Sharron Stockhausen and Expert Publishing. Their service and support has been just amazing. They know their stuff, and they do it well. Thank you, friends, for helping me bring this little book into the world.

Cindy Greenwood is one of the best HR professionals I have worked with. She is also one of those friends who will tell me, "Yes, those jeans make you look fat." Thank you, Cindy, for reading my manuscript draft and providing such helpful, constructive feedback. You are still one of my best hires!

Acknowledgements

Jody Lessard taught me how to find more balance in my life and showed me that my success is influenced by my health. She showed me the importance of aligning strength and stamina with heart and soul. (Anyone who can convince me that running a 5K is a good and fun thing to do is just absolutely amazing!) Thank you, Jody.

My sisters, Julie Benedict and Lori Charron... Where do I even start! You just fill my life with joy. You continue to help me become the person I dream of being—accepting me where I'm at while encouraging me to expand my vision of success and significance. There is no one on this earth who I love laughing with more than you guys. You are just stinkin' fun!

And my husband, Steve. You taught me it was OK to be authentic. And you have shown me it's possible to be passionate and committed to my work without letting it take over my life. That's a big lesson for me. You show me more grace and mercy than I deserve. You are my wonderful.

Introduction

*I*t's 8:00 a.m. Monday morning. You're usually picking up your blueberry bagel and latte on the way to work. But today is different. There's no place to go. You don't have a job. You are unemployed.

The good news? Millions of people are having the same experience. The bad news? Millions of people are having the same experience. (I wonder if the bagel bakers have noticed a decrease in sales.) Your job search may have been kick-started because of a layoff, a firing, or you simply got tired of your boss yelling at you and you decided to quit. Whichever the reason, you want to be smart about your job search. You're ready to get started. *And you need to stand out.*

This little book is designed to give you a crash course in the activities most important to finding a new job—things like creating a strategy, networking, writing a resume, dealing with your emotions, using good research, interviewing, taking care of yourself, and staying focused. It's written so you can quickly go to any chapter/topic, choose the suggestions that work best for you, and then put them into action. Consider it your how-to manual.

Keep the book handy—by your telephone or computer as a quick reference for writing resumes or preparing for interviews. Or carry it in your briefcase, purse, or interview notebook for encouragement before a key networking conversation or when writing a thank-you note. It is *your* little book for big success.

Every author faces the dilemma on how to handle pronouns. You and I both know the world of job seekers, recruiters, and hiring managers includes men and women. Out of respect for you the reader and for everyone who's ever been involved in a job search, I use both male and female pronouns throughout the book. That means you'll get examples from both perspectives, which is how life really is.

If you have lost your job as a result of a downsizing or restructuring, you will find some of the examples speak directly to your situation. My heart goes out to you who have been told "your position isn't needed anymore." You may understand in your head that eliminating your position is a business decision. But it hurts in your heart. It *is* personal. My wish is this book will help you get back on your feet quickly and you'll land the job of your dreams!

The end of a job signals the start of something new. And with new beginnings, there is *hope*. May you find some of that in this little book for big success!

Chapter 1

A $20 Bill is Still a $20 Bill After It's Been Through the Wash

You are Significant

"*W*here do you work?" "What do you do?" "How's work going?" When you are unemployed, these questions can make you feel like you've lost the ability to speak in complete sentences and your mouth has filled with cotton. Instead of feeling like the competent, smart adult you are, you're back in first grade. Mrs. Nelson is calling on you and you forgot to do the assignment.

This deer in headlights reaction usually appears because it's just hard to say you're unemployed. You may find it (unfortunately) a little embarrassing. Your self worth is easily tied to your position or title. When that validation goes away, you may question your own abilities and contributions. So remember this: your layoff or unemployment does not define you. It does not determine your worth. Just as a run through the washing machine doesn't decrease the value of a $20 bill, unemployment doesn't decrease *your* value. Nothing about *you* has changed, except you are no longer working for the company that once employed you. You are a person with emotions, talents, and life experiences. *You are significant.*

———— . ————

You are Significant

Don't confuse your job with who you are as a person. You may be the Grand Pooh-Bah of All Things Important at ABC Corporation. Or you're the unemployed marketing manager spending thirteen hours a week sending out resumes. The title doesn't matter. You are a person with values, dreams, and goals. Your job is just one way you live out who you are. You are significant because you were created with talents and skills and abilities that are uniquely yours. You still have them, even if you are unemployed. You were created for a purpose no one else can fulfill. No one else can be you. And *that* makes you significant.

While you're looking for a job, take time each day to read, meditate, or pray. Be silent. Consider and be grateful for all the good things you have in your life. You have a special place in this world. Your life matters.

Getting Started

First things first. Get your head and emotions in the game. Your first impulse may be to pull out the old resume and add your most recent job to it. That's *one* way of beginning your transition, but it's not the *best* way.

The best way? Begin to work through the emotions. It's most likely you're experiencing guilt, anxiety, and fear. Common reactions. If you don't take time to think about them now, and instead start right in on tasks (updating the resume), in a very short time you're going to short-circuit. Your heart and your feelings won't keep up with the mental and physical work you're trying to accomplish. So first, take a deep breath. Talk with your friends. Take a long walk. Sit and think or meditate. Refuse to be motivated by fear. Instead, be motivated by the potential new opportunities in front of you.

During these first few days, take time to adjust to your transition. Your schedule is totally out of whack, your daily routine has been interrupted, and you have no place you have to be tomorrow morning. This isn't the time to make important decisions. And it's not the time to send out hundreds of resumes. Take time to consider what just happened to you, grieve the loss of your job, and focus on what comes next.

When you're ready to begin thinking about your next job—and before you update your resume—ask yourself four important questions:

1. When I consider all the jobs I've ever had, what did I enjoy most?
2. If I have a choice (and you do!), what work do I not want to repeat?
3. What work environment was a good fit for me (the physical office space, energy of the work team, privacy, noise level, location, etc.)?
4. What three things are most important to me in my next job?

Dr. Howard Thurman was an influential philosopher, educator, and civil rights activist. His advice is so relevant to the job seeker: "Don't ask yourself what the world needs. Ask yourself what makes you come alive and then go do it. Because what the world needs is people who have come alive."

**A $20 bill is still a $20 bill
after it's been through the wash.**

Chapter 2

Scream in Your Pillow or Buy a Punching Bag

Work Through Your Emotions

You remember walking into the conference room and seeing your boss and the human resources manager sitting there. You knew it couldn't be good. You heard the words, "Your job has been eliminated." And then everything went silent. You could see the HR manager was still talking. Her lips were moving, but in slow motion. Your boss didn't even look at you. You had to remind yourself to breathe. There is no sound, only the roar of silence in your head.

Your frustration, anger, and hurt over being laid off are understandable. You have the right to feel betrayed. You may understand in your head that it's a business decision. But it still hurts in your heart. It *is* personal. So *work through your emotions*. Scream in your pillow. Buy a punching bag. Run until your legs can't run anymore. Cry with a good friend or let off steam with the guys. Release your frustration and get your anger under control. And then move on. Hanging on to your anger will only cripple your job-seeking efforts. Move through your pain.

———— · ————

Moving Through the Ups and Downs

This is a tough time. And anyone who tells you differently just doesn't get it. Yes, losing your job presents new opportunities and a chance to re-evaluate what's important to you. But it still hurts.

Do you remember riding the roller coaster at the fair when you were younger? The faster, the better. And if you felt like throwing up when it was all over, you knew you'd gotten your money's worth. It just didn't get any better than that, right? The ride usually began with a slow, bumpy, upward crawl at a ninety degree angle (I called it the "death march"). You didn't question whether the rickety wooden planks would keep your car on the tracks. You just kept waiting for the inevitable sudden drop in altitude. And then you felt it. The plunge left your heart and stomach at the top of the loop while your body pitched forward. As a symbol of your bravery, you raised your arms in the air and celebrated being alive. The twists, the turns, the spirals, the ups, the downs—half the time you wondered if you were going to die, and the rest of the time you believed you were going to die!

Your emotions during this transition are going to feel the same way. You should expect to experience anger, shock, disappointment, resentment, and acceptance. It is normal to go through the blues, depression, high energy, low energy, and anxiety. So what do you do about these ups and downs? You move up and down! And eventually you find the way that works for you to regain some of your equilibrium.

Stuffing your emotions won't get you anywhere. Ignoring them will either a) make you physically sick with stress-related illnesses, or b) cause you to lose it at the wrong time with the wrong person (like during an interview). Your responsibility is to identify what's going on in your head and your heart, and figure out how to move to a better place.

One Thing at a Time

"I realized my teams back at my place of employment had moved on without me. I also knew I was starting to run out of names to contact. Now I have started to hit the blues and the depressing thoughts came in. I skipped them initially because I started my search so aggressively."

~ Tim R.

Overwhelmed. That seems to be the word/emotion used most frequently with job seekers, especially during the first few weeks of unemployment. So many things have changed. You feel the tension and frustration in your head, your stomach, your heart, and your soul. "What am I supposed to do? What do I do first?" And after that first rush of panic, the big deal questions start. These are the ones that could keep you in bed for the next three months if you let them be your center of attention: "What about our mortgage? What if we can't afford Susie's piano lessons? What about our vacation plans? What if my wife loses her job, too? What if we lose our health insurance? What if no one ever hires me again?"

These "what if" questions are guaranteed to keep your heart racing, your blood pressure rising, and your stomach churning unless you choose to stop for a moment and keep your life in perspective.

Here are six things you can do right away that will help you feel productive and gain some equilibrium:

- Move. Take a walk. Get some physical activity. Work out that tension in your stomach and shoulders.
- Communicate. Talk with your family about your job search and how you're feeling. Keep them informed.
- Reach out. Ask for help. Let people encourage you. Don't interpret their support as pity.
- Budget. Start thinking about how you can cut back on expenses.
- Plan. Create a job search strategy. Plan your work and work your plan.
- Vent. A hiring manager can see a chip on your shoulder from a mile away. Get rid of your anger and tension before you interview.

If you are eligible for unemployment, this is a good time to contact your local unemployment office and get that paperwork started. And check out what resources are available to you through workforce centers in your community. I have identified a few links in the resource list at the end of this book that could be helpful.

Take a deep breath and remember to exhale. The only thing that has happened right now is you are temporarily out of work. Take some time to just work through this experience. The other issues will be addressed as you create your job search strategy, work your plan consistently, and adjust your lifestyle as necessary. Focus on one thing at a time.

> "The most important thing to me during my job search was the faith I had in knowing God had better plans for me. I just had to do my part to figure out where He wanted me."
>
> ~ Sue K.

I believe that a pint of chocolate chip Haagen Dazs ice cream, Diet Pepsi, my navy blue sweat pants, and watching TV reruns of James Garner in *The Rockford Files* can make any bad day seem better. (If you are too young to know who James Garner is…well, I'm sorry about that.) Eventually, I know I need to put the ice cream spoon down and return to the land of the living and employed. If I stay in my pity place too long, I won't get what I want. I'm only going to get fat and lazy.

Give yourself some time to adjust to your new reality. Then start looking ahead. There are good things in store for you.

Work through your emotions.

Appoint Yourself CEO
Create a Good Support Team

Y ou've always wanted to run your own business, be the one in charge, Mr. or Ms. Important, the ruler over all decisions. Well this is your chance. You are the CEO of your own newly formed company—John Doe Finds a Job. And now you need an advisory board. *Put together your own board of directors.* Who can advise you, coach you, challenge you, and encourage you? Surround yourself with people (business colleagues, friends, and family) who will provide resources and connections during this time of transition. Pull your team together, listen to their advice, and enjoy the results.

Fire the Dead Weight

Resentment, pride, and guilt are three ugly friends you don't want in your new company. They keep you focused inward. They give you permission to stay in a high level of anxiety and prevent you from making choices that will help you find a job. Fire them! Kick them off the train and tear up their round-trip tickets.

People Want to Help

You do not have to face this transition alone. People want to help. Yes, asking for help may be a new experience for you. This isn't the time to be Wonder Woman or Super Man.

Create your own board of directors. This is the group that will share your celebrations and your discouragements. These are people you already know and like. They are people you trust. People you know care about you.

Choosing the Right People

Your board of directors is a group of five to seven people committed to supporting you during your job search. Include people who will support you *and* speak the truth to you. You want them to question your strategies, challenge your decisions, and encourage your spirit.

Remember that it can be difficult for those closest to you to tell you things you may not want to hear. They want you to move *away* from your pain. And you're looking for a board of directors that will help you move *through* the pain. Choose people that will give you smart business perspectives with heart-healthy sensitivity.

Their commitment: listen, advise, and encourage.

Your commitment: keep them updated on your search—the bad news and the good news.

Creating your Board of Directors

1. Identify five to seven people who care about you and you can depend on.

   One of them could be your spouse/partner. The others may be former co-workers, close friends, people you've worked with on committees, and/or people with whom you volunteer or worship. The one thing they all have in common is they care about *you*.

2. Call them and ask them to help. Say something like this:

   "Hello, Mary? This is John. You've probably heard I'm no longer with ABC Corporation and I'm looking for a new job. I'm asking a few people to serve as an advisory group for me during this transition—kind of like a board of directors. Can I tell you a little bit about this? See if you might be willing to help me out? Great!

"Here's what I'm looking for. I'm putting together a group of about six people that can advise me, listen to me, and encourage me. We may get together a couple times as a group, but it's more likely that we'll talk individually on the phone every couple weeks. I'll keep you updated on my job search. I'd especially appreciate your advice on my strategy and action steps, and your help in making good networking connections. And probably most important, I need the group to keep me focused on what I need to do to find my next job and encourage me when I need it.

"I'm inviting this group out for coffee next Saturday morning. I can tell you more about my job search plan, and get some good advice from all of you then. Are you up for this? Thanks, Mary."

3. Call or email them regularly.

Call at least three members of your board of directors every week. (Include this as an action item in your Weekly Plan for Success.) Tell them your goals for the week. Ask them for advice. Tell them how you're feeling.

Let them know what connections you're trying to make. Be specific. Ask them if there is anyone in their network who might have connections to the companies, industry leaders, or association members you're trying to reach.

Create a board of directors' email distribution list. Email them when you've got an interview coming up. Email them when you get one of those disappointing "no thank you" letters. Email them when you've got a new lead—they may be able to add to it.

4. Always say thank you.

   This group shouldn't expect anything in return for serving on your board. If they do, you may want to un-invite them. But a nice thank-you email for a piece of advice or new connection is always appreciated. When a company has made the smart decision to hire you, invite them out for coffee or lunch as a way of saying thanks. Then tell them about your new job!

   If someone seems reluctant to commit, graciously offer them a way out. "You know, Dave, it sounds like you've already got a full plate. I know that you're there if I need you. Rather than being a part of this group, maybe I can just check in with you once in awhile." Chances are Dave will be grateful for your sensitivity, no damage has been done to the rela tionship, and you've got someone else to reach out to on an as-needed basis.

Connecting with members of your board of directors doesn't always need to be over the phone or around the table. One job seeker I know scheduled time each week to walk with one of her advisory team members. Twice around the shopping mall (weather was never an excuse) and she was energized with new ideas and helpful feedback.

This group of people will embrace the opportunity to help and support you. I'm not kidding. If they've agreed to be on your board, you know they care about you and your future. Consider their advice, respect their time, and watch for opportunities to give back to them.

Your are the CEO of your job search.
Put together a top-notch board of directors.

Chapter 4

Play with a Yo-Yo

Prepare a Resume That Makes You Stand Out

*R*emember the yo-yo? It's the round toy with a string attached and the toy is spun up and down the string from your hand. You probably played with one when you were a kid. Try it again—notice how quickly the skill comes back. Forgot you could do that, didn't you! *Take time to consider all your skills and accomplishments as you prepare or update your resume.* Things that come naturally to you shouldn't be dismissed. Make sure you include yo-yo's you used in previous jobs. Do a wide-sweep inventory of what you enjoy doing—your skills, talents, and interests. Capture them in your primary marketing tool, your resume. *Make yourself stand out.*

Resume Format and Content

Your resume is your marketing brochure. Its purpose? Get you noticed so you're invited for an interview. It will tell potential employers about your work history, skills, education, and relevant professional information. It should also give them a little insight into your personality and work style. Most importantly, it should very easily and quickly make the connection between their needs and what you have to offer. Catch their interest!

There's no right way to format a resume. Different formats highlight different parts of your background. Keep in mind that unless you are applying for a very creative position in a creative agency, you will want to keep the flash and graphic sizzle out of your resume. Always give the impression that says, "I'm a professional, I'm very good at what I do, and I can do the job you're hiring for."

So what's included in a resume?

- Contact information at the top of the first page. Keep in mind that you want to present yourself professionally. If your email address says otherwise, e.g., **HotBabe@email.com**, try something more professional until you find a job.

- Professional Profile or Professional Summary. I suggest using a Professional Profile rather than a Career Objective. Why? The Career Objective says more about what *you're* interested in, than it does about selling what you can do for the company. Your Profile should include words and phrases that highlight the best of what you bring to the table—your accomplishments, professional roles, and strengths. It's a brief, one-paragraph introduction. Be creative—this is where some of your personality can shine through.

- Experience
  - ⇨ Company
  - ⇨ Dates of employment (start with your most recent position)
  - ⇨ Job title
  - ⇨ Accomplishments
  - ⇨ Make sure you include your skills and experience that align with what the potential employer wants

- Education
  - ⇨ College, vocational training, specialized courses or training
  - ⇨ Include current certifications here, especially if they are relevant to the position you're applying for

- Other information that captures the reader's attention and helps her get to know you
  - ⇨ Military service
  - ⇨ Boards you have served on
  - ⇨ Associations / Memberships

⇨ Languages
⇨ Community volunteer activities
⇨ Interesting accomplishments (i.e., note that you've climbed a mountain or completed a triathlon. If I'd done either of those things I'd probably plaster it all over the front page and send out the news in a mass mailing.)

Any reference to salary is best saved until a second or third interview. Don't include it in your resume.

Notice the phrase "References available upon request" is not included in your resume. That's expected—you will provide references when they are requested. Your references should be neatly typed on one sheet of paper. Use the same heading as your resume (your name and contact information), and provide the contact information (phone and email addresses) for each reference. It's also a good idea to include one or two sentences that describe your professional relationship with each reference. For example:

Jane Doe, Vice President for Finance, ABC
Corporation
123-456-7890
Jane@emailaddress.com

Jane was my supervisor at ABC Corporation for five years. She can specifically speak to my ability to lead a team through a system conversion.

Ask permission from your list of references *before* you send their names and information to any potential employer.

Developing Your Resume

Knowing that your resume may get only a brief review, keep these points in mind:

- Easy to read; no clutter
- No more than two pages
- Contact information at the top (name, address, phone, email)
- Professional font; 12 pt. font size
- Use bullets to capture your accomplishments
- Don't include references
- List ten to fifteen years of employment history
- Ensure that your resume highlights what the employer is looking for
- Use information from the job posting to tailor your resume
- Tell the truth; don't exaggerate
- Proofread, proofread, proofread

You will find an example of a typical resume format at the end of this chapter. You can also download it at **http://www.SignificantSolutionsInc.com/Big-Success.html**. Remember though, you want to tell your story well—and the typical format may not always accomplish that. Consider these alternatives:

- If there is a significant gap in your work history, address it in one or two sentences in your cover letter. If the primary reason for the gap is because you haven't been able to find a job, identify how you're filling that gap—volunteering, taking classes, developing workshops in your area of expertise, etc.

- If you've taken a survival job while you continue to look for something that aligns with your career goals, make sure your resume focuses on the work most relevant to the position you're applying for. Don't lead with your survival job if it doesn't sell the depth and breadth of your skills. Consider replacing the "Experience" heading with a focused heading that sells your professional experience, i.e., Financial Analyst Experience, listing only relevant positions. Then use an Other Work section to list your survival job and other gap-filling positions. Or create a Key Strengths or Career Summary section before listing your work experience.

- If you are changing career paths, you will need to paint a very clear picture for the reader about your ability to be successful in the job you're applying for. For instance, if you have decided to follow your dream of becoming a teacher after twenty years of selling insurance, you need to clearly articulate how your sales experience and financial/business acumen have prepared you for the academic world. Position your resume so it sells your ability to work with people, your strong communication skills, creativity in teaching, experience working with youth or adult learners, and other professional skills and talents that will tell your story well. Format the resume and highlight the experiences that capture the recruiter's interest. In a situation like this, I strongly encourage you to network with professionals in your new industry. Ask them to review your resume and give you constructive feedback.

> "When I got laid off, I put my resume on six job boards. Most of the responses came from job placement agencies. I was told that many times placement agencies will post a nonexistent job so they will have candidates in the pipeline when a client needs someone with those skills."
>
> ~ Sandie T.

Oops! What Happened Here?

Earlier in my career I was the corporate employment manager at a large financial institution. I received a letter and resume from a candidate that provides an example of what *not* to do. (I'm including it without making corrections.)

"Dear Personnel Manager:

I'm looking for a position in the mergers and acquisitions department. You have anyone retiring in that departmet [sic] during the next decade? Have a nice day."

The letter certainly captured my attention. But unfortunately, it wasn't for the right reasons. I ventured into the attached resume. The Career Objective listed:

"To be incorporated in the business administration position, hopefully in the marketing department."

Didn't he say he was looking for something in mergers and acquisitions?

And if that wasn't enough to tell me he wasn't the right fit for the job, his resume included a section called "Resume Plus:"

"Can read write and speak spanish its as good as receiving a MBA in it [sic]."

Wow. I must admit I felt sorry for the guy. I wonder where he ended up working. It wasn't for us.

Getting Your Resume Noticed for the Right Reasons

Your resume is your calling card. It is usually the first piece of written information a potential employer gets on you. It creates the first impression. Make it look good.

Every hiring manager and HR recruiter has her own way of evaluating resumes. Whichever method is chosen, you know some resumes will be considered more closely, and others will get set aside—each resume getting *maybe* ten seconds of attention. When I'm reviewing resumes, I usually sort them into three piles: A, B, and C. The A pile includes those resumes that have caught my interest and appear to meet the minimum requirements we're hiring for. I will go back and look at them more closely later. The B pile includes resumes I have some question on—they'll get a second look if my A pile doesn't give me what we need. The C pile includes resumes that are clearly not a good fit for the presentation. I don't look at them again.

The best way to get your resume into the A pile? Make the connection between your experience and skills and the employer's needs and wants. Be interesting. Highlight your accomplishments. Make the reader want to know more about you. And the best way to get into the C pile? Misspell words, use incorrect grammar, punctuation, or capitalization, and focus on what *you're* looking for in a job, not what the potential employer needs.

Highlight your accomplishments. What most people include in their work history is a list of responsibilities or job description duties. Why doesn't that work? It doesn't tell the hiring manager whether or not you can *do* those things. The reader wants to know how you're going to help them be more successful. So tell them. List your accomplishments.

Accomplishments

In your resume you're going to list the companies you've worked for and positions you've held for the last ten to fifteen years. Under each position, highlight what you did for the company that contributed to its success. When possible, use numbers; percentages; words like decreased, increased, changed, improved, etc. to indicate your work made a difference.

On my website you can download a document that will help you write your accomplishments in a way that captures the reader's attention. Go to **http://www.SignificantSolutionsInc.com/BigSuccess.html.**

Try Something Different

Two points to keep in mind:

1) You want to get noticed.
2) You want the potential employer to know you can do the job.

In addition to networking and submitting your resume, what else can you do to draw attention to your skills and experience?

Mark B. added two more activities to his job search strategy. He is a very creative individual with experience in engineering and as a machinist. When he talks about his job search, he reminds the listener, "Not only can I think outside the box, but I can also build the box." That gets their attention. In one instance, Mark first identified a target company he wanted to work with. Finding their product page on the Internet, he replicated the product site and added pictures of his inventions to it. Very clever. Another business owner spent several hours talking with Mark about his proposal for expanding their market to the Midwest. Mark's professional and well-articulated ideas caught their attention. He knew their product line, he had the technical skills, he was thinking creatively, and he made a good business case for his idea. Who knows where this key connection will lead?

Proofread, Proofread, Proofread

When I was in high school, I took a class in which we created a skills-training model office. Each of us was assigned to a position. I was Clerk Typist I. (Keep in mind that this was before computers were part of the classroom. We used typewriters and carbon paper. Yeah, I know, hard to believe.) At the end of each day, I received an A or an F on my work. If my work was perfect—no misspelled words, typos, or grammatical errors—I received an A. If I had even one mistake in my work, I received an F. Sounds pretty terrible, right? It prepared me very well for the future. When I worked as director of human resources for a Fortune 500 company, the senior vice president gave our team very specific instructions. "Never send me your homework. Give me your final product." He appropriately demanded our A work.

Your resume deserves the same strict discipline. Proofread it several times. Then have someone else proof it. Use the spell check on your computer. (But realize it's only checking your spelling. It doesn't know if you meant to write "to" or "too.") If you have time, set your resume aside for a few hours or until the next day. Then go back and look at it with a fresh perspective.

And Remember

You're going to get disappointing news and encouraging news once you start applying for positions. And it's likely you will receive more "Thank you and good luck" responses than "You're the one we want!" Bummer. You are making yourself vulnerable every time you send out your resume. So remember. Your unemployment doesn't define you. You are a person of worth. Work through your emotions, take time for hobbies and activities that bring you joy, and stick to your job search plan. This won't last forever.

Take time to consider all your skills and accomplishments as you prepare your resume. Make yourself stand out.

Mike Jones

123 – First Avenue North
Anywhere, MN 12345

(H) 123-456-7899
(C) 987-654-3211
MikeJones@email.net

Professional Profile

Top performer with over 22 years experience in the food industry. Exceptional customer service skills have been recognized by customers, vendors, and colleagues. Demonstrated success in increasing retail sales and produce management. Self-motivated, personable, and committed to creating long-term customer relationships.

Experience

Super Company   **5/06 – 2/09**

Produce Team Lead

- Managed produce team of five (including hiring, training, and coaching)
- Increased 2007 YTD sales by 16% over the previous year
- Led the district in guest service and produce freshness scores
- Managed inventory control through effective and efficient ordering
- Maintained ad pricing and price changes
- Provided guests with prompt and courteous service

Your Best Food Market   5/02 – 5/06

Assistant Grocery Manager
Interim Produce Manager
Pricing Coordinator and Produce Assistant Manager

- Managed store operations; store generated $80,000 monthly revenue
- Negotiated pricing and in-store promotional items with vendors
- Managed computerized pricing system
- Prepared weekly food sales advertisements
- Prepared merchandise displays

Food Store   12/99 – 5/02

Lead Sales Rep
Produce Sales Rep

- Consistently exceeded sales goals: 13.5% over current budgeted year; 11.6% over previous year
- Consistently sold add-ons
- Effectively negotiated prices resulting in annual invoice cost adjustments of 2%
- Efficiently verified direct confirmations, made adjustments, and prepared billing

Retail For You   12/95 – 12/99

Assistant Store Sales Manager

- Consistently exceeded store and individual sales goals by providing excellent customer service and utilizing innovative merchandising

- Prepared sales forecasts and monthly sales plan
- Presented and demonstrated new products
- Managed inventory and point of sale systems
- Trained associates

Education

Associate of Applied Science Degree

- Anywhere Community College
- Business and Marketing Emphasis

Honors

- Three-time recipient of Food Store's Bonus Program
- Your Best Food Market District Safety Award

Volunteer Activities / Additional Information

- Habitat for Humanity volunteer
- Volunteer softball coach for Anywhere Middle School
- Speak conversational Spanish
- Completed Grandma's Marathon

Chapter 5

Call Aunt Betty and Uncle Earl and Cousin Ed and...

Network, Network, Network

It's all about networking. So make a list of one hundred people you know. That's right—one hundred. You may have worked with the people on your list, they may be related to you, they wait on you in your favorite restaurant, they used to be your boss, they sit next to you in church, they groom your dog. You get the idea. Tell them about your job search. Ask them for help. And always, always, always say thank you, and watch for the opportunity to return the favor.

So what is Networking?

You're probably already tired of hearing about networking. "You've got to network!" "Who's in your network?" "The only way to find a job is by networking!" "Who have you networked with this week?" "Have you tried social networking?" "What networking support group do you belong to?" Blah, blah, blah. Well, here's the deal. As tired as you are of hearing about networking, it's still the best way to find a job. And it needs to be an important part of your job search strategy.

"Yeah, right," you might be muttering under your breath. "But I don't like selling myself." "It's just not me." "That's not my style." "I'm not outgoing enough." These reactions are understandable and are a good reminder we need to be clear on what it means to network.

Networking is simply a process people use to help each other out. It's built on a relationship. It's not about selling anything. And you don't have to be the life of the party to do it well.

Several years ago I attended a leadership luncheon at the University of Minnesota. It was a business attire event with an impressive keynote speaker. In other words, you showed up knowing you'd be rubbing shoulders with some corporate super stars. I got to my assigned seat and noticed one of my table partners had already placed his business card on each one of our plates. Bad idea. Before sitting

down I had already determined that I wasn't interested in networking with this guy. Not only had he
prematurely assumed I wanted to get to know him,
he came across looking like a slick sales guy with
an ego that screamed, "It's all about me!" Unfortunately, his table conversation confirmed my first
impression. I'm quite certain his name wasn't added
to a lot of address books that day.

Here's what the guy missed: networking is a
two-way street. It's about the other person *and*
it's about you. It's based on a relationship. People
network with people they know and like. It isn't
just about handing out your business cards or seeing how many names you can get added to your
LinkedIn site.

Build and Nurture the Relationship

People love talking about themselves. So let them
do it. Find something they're interested in and let
them tell you about it. Ask open-ended questions—
questions that can't be answered with a yes or no.
You want to engage in a conversation. Three safe
and smart areas to focus on when learning about
someone: family, work, and hobbies. Ask a question and see where it takes you. If the conversation
dies, ask another question. The more you let the
other guy talk, the more interesting he will find you
(seems backwards, doesn't it?), and the more he will
like you because you're interested in the same things

he is! The more he likes you, the more energy he'll put into helping you find a job. It's funny how that works.

> "Network groups are a little like mini counseling sessions. They get you out of the house, away from the computer, and require you to be disciplined to be at a certain place at a certain time. I received first-hand advice, links into all kinds of job search tools, and connections to helpful organizations. After what felt like being dumped out on the street by my former employer, it seemed like I was picked up by this amazing garbage truck that would help and carry me all the way to my next job destination. I was totally amazed at how supportive and helpful a bunch of strangers in the same room were towards me and one another. I feel honored to have met some really good people."
>
> ~ Ian T.

How to Begin

Let's go back to that list of one hundred people you've created. These are people who can help you make connections. Connections to other people, to companies, to associations, and perhaps to jobs. Create a system that collects their contact information, helps you track your conversations with them, and reminds you to follow-up. Some of you may already have your list of one hundred included in another contact database such as Outlook or ACT. Make whatever system tweaks are necessary to tag these contacts as part of your strategic job search network. If an electronic tracking system doesn't work for you, just use a 3-ring binder. (A 3-ring binder also gives you a place to store other relevant job search information.) Use one sheet of paper for each person on your networking list. Insert the pages alphabetically by last name so you can quickly and easily find a contact. Write their contact information under their names, and make notes of conversations you have with them (include the dates).

What to do with Your List of One Hundred Contacts

1. Identify your networking goals.

   - Do you want connections to a specific industry? Company? Board of directors?
   - Do you want advice on what companies to seek out?
   - Are you looking for someone who can give you feedback on your resume or job search strategy?
   - Are you looking for informational interviews?

   Most likely, you'll want to include all of the above, and other goals important to your search.

2. Start with the first person on your list of one hundred.

- Let's say his name is Todd. Determine which networking goal Todd can help you out with. Decide if it's best to call, email, or meet with Todd. Schedule this activity on your calendar. Plan it.
- Ask Todd what's going on in his life. Be interested. Listen for ways you can help *him* network. What connections or resources can you point in his direction?
- How can Todd help you? If it's not clear he's connected to a company or individual you'd like to reach out to, then simply tell him you're looking for a new job.
- Be clear about what you're asking for. Try not to use the phrase, "Do you know of any job openings for a financial analyst?" Chances are he doesn't. (People don't generally know about job openings. But they *do* know people who are connected to places that might have job openings.) Instead, say, "Todd, I'm looking for a job as a financial analyst. Do you know anyone who could help me move forward in my job search? Perhaps someone who works at a financial institution?"
- If Todd has a connection that's important to you, then ask for specific help. "If I remember correctly, Todd, you worked at ABC Fi-

nancial Company a few years ago. I'd love to talk to someone there about their business. Who do you suggest I talk to?" (Notice that you didn't say you wanted to ask someone for a job. You're simply asking Todd to make a connection for you. You want to build a relationship with this new contact.) If Todd gives you a name, ask him for the best way to reach this new contact and for permission to mention his name.

- Follow-up with the new connection(s).
- Send Todd a thank-you note for giving you the referral, and keep him posted on your job search.

3. Go to the next person on your list of one hundred and repeat Step 2.

4. Repeat Step 3 until everyone on your list of one hundred has been contacted. Remember to keep notes on your conversations with Todd and your new connections in your network tracking system/3-ring binder.

Remember, you want to make yourself stand out. Your posted resume on a job search board like monster.com is competing with hundreds of other people looking for a new opportunity. When you are able to connect with a person—a living, breathing, human being who knows you—your competition is reduced to a very small number. You may be the only candidate in that pool.

"Even though finances were tight because of my recent layoff, my hair still needed to be cut. Maggie has been cutting my hair for years and she knew I was having a bad day. I told her about my layoff. She told me to give her a copy of my resume. I wondered why. I'm not looking for a job in a salon or as a stylist. She persisted, and I finally got her a resume from my car. The next day she called. Her neighbor is the CEO of a company who was looking for an executive with my background. Can you believe that? I got the job! I always thought you had to network with people from your own profession or industry. I was wrong. You never know who knows whom. My advice? Talk to everyone you know about your job search. It works."

~ Corrine L.

Social Networking

If you're looking for a job, you're in sales. And a successful sales strategy requires a marketing plan. What are you marketing? You, your experience, skills, and attitude. Use a variety of ways to get your information out to the market, including social networking.

Social networking builds online communities of people. You choose your social network service(s) and communicate and interact with friends, family, and others with similar interests. (Facebook, LinkedIn, and Twitter are examples of common networking communities.) These sites give you the opportunity to create your own marketing material. You get to decide how to talk about your skills, adventures, dreams, experiences, and goals. Your pictures make it easy to make a connection with your online community. And even better, social networking reaches an audience that is larger and more diverse than any audience you can reach using your address book and mass mailing a one-page marketing flyer.

Recruiters and hiring managers are using these online billboards to learn more about candidates even before interviews are scheduled. So remember you want to present a profile that says "I'm ready to work, energetic, smart, and the kind of person you'd like to know more about."

Although it may be fun to post the picture of you and your outrageous friends enjoying the nightlife, remember who else is looking at these sites. You may want to put your Cancun pictures back up after you've landed your job. Your blogging and Twitter conversations could very likely be used as part of the vetting process by potential employers before they've even contacted you. Choose your billboard words wisely during your job search.

"One of the biggest helps to me during my job search was Pastor Rod Anderson's Job Transition Group. The number of people there who knew someone, someplace, who could be a contact for me helped make my search exciting. Without those contacts and being able to actually talk to someone at a company I applied at through the Internet, it would have been a very depressing job search.

"I landed my job (after working at my former company for twenty-two-plus years) because I emailed my resume to someone that I worked with twelve years ago. My resume got passed on in the company and landed on the right desk at the right time. It is all about networking. (And when you write down all the people you know, you have a much larger network than you think.)"

~ Sue K.

Networking Like a Pro

My friend PK Ziaja is the best networker I know. She has an ever-growing list of contacts that covers an amazing array of industries, businesses, and organizational levels. But the size of her list is not what makes her so good at networking. What makes her stand out is how she respects and cultivates her connections. She stays in touch. She sends notes and birthday cards. She remembers your family. She keeps her commitments. She follows through and follows-up. She always makes it about the other person. And she's good at what she does. Whether it's for business referrals, employment opportunities, or fund raising, PK doesn't connect people simply because she can. She connects them because she has done her homework—she knows the people and she knows their needs. She watches for opportunities to make connections, and as a result, her own business grows. (You really want to be in PK's rolodex.)

"Always begin the connection with 'How can I help you?' Then listen and seek to understand. Once you have learned how you can help someone else, they will naturally ask how they can help you. Strive to be purposeful and succinct in explaining what you need so they have a clear understanding of your request.

"Make it easy for the other person to help you in your job search. For example, if you are asking Billie to introduce you to Sam, a potential employment contact, craft the message for Billie. Keep it to three points: 1) What you do; 2) How Sam can help you; 3) Why Sam should care about helping you. Billie can then email or call Sam and make the introduction for you efficiently and easily."

~ PK Ziaja

**You can talk about networking
or you can network.**

**Talk to people.
And if that doesn't work, talk to more people.**

Chapter 6

Wear a Sherlock Holmes Cap and Grab a Magnifying Glass

Do Your Research

*S*herlock Holmes, move over! This is the opportunity for you to play the starring role in your own detective series. Find out what's happening in your industry. What are the trends? What companies do you want to work for? Check them out. Talk to the experts. Google. Read the business journals. Make notes. Draw conclusions and form opinions. Be prepared. *Research, research, research.*

Focus Your Research

One of the positive results of being unemployed (and yes, there are a few), is the time you've been given to *focus* on your search. And this focus and your strategy need to include research activities. If you love to sit in front of the computer and surf the net from sunup to sundown, you're going to love this part!

There are three key areas to research:

- Your industry or the industry you want to work in,
- Companies you are interested in working for,
- Contacts in these industries and companies.

Before you start Googling the day away, set up a system that will help you capture all the good data you're going to discover. My suggestion: set up a file on your computer called My Job Search. (I'll talk more about this later in chapter 9.) This main file is where you will keep all other job search files—keeping you organized and reducing your stress. One of your job search files should be called Research. As you research, create files here where you can collect the data you find. If you aren't setting up an electronic system, include a Research section in your 3-ring binder.

Remember, your focus is on finding a job. If you find you've researched your way into areas that have taken you way off course and three hours have passed since you last took your eyes off your computer screen, take a pause. Don't get buried in interesting but not helpful minutiae. Be strategic about your research. Use your time wisely. If you find a site or topic that interests you but is not relevant to finding a job, note the link in a miscellaneous research file and go back to it later.

Industry Research

Stay current on what's happening in your profession and industry. You want to go into your next interview demonstrating you haven't missed a beat during your transition. You know what's going on in your business. You're sharp. You're prepared. The Internet is a powerful tool for research. So is the library. Use them to study industry journals, periodicals, and business newspapers that can keep you up to date on industry trends, challenges, shake-ups, and successes.

Company Research

Make a list of the companies you're interested in. Then start checking them out—electronically and at the library. How are they doing financially? Any recent changes in leadership? If so, how might that change the way they do business? (A great interview question for you to ask.) How have recent economic changes affected them and their competitors? What does their website say? This is their primary marketing tool—study it. What are respected industry bloggers saying about the company? Read company press releases and annual reports. Dunn and Bradstreet, Hoovers Business Directory, and the U.S. Securities and Exchange Commission are excellent business resources. And don't forget the business section of your local newspaper.

Here's another suggestion. If you aren't sure where to look for relevant information and you are determined to stay in front of your computer rather than venture out of the house, call your local library. The reference librarians know their stuff. Ask them to help you get started. Who knows? You may discover your library has a really neat coffee shop, the personal assistance is helpful, and it's a great place to spend a couple hours working on your research.

Contact Research

Network, network, network. Contact research is the step that will broaden your networking base. It will tell you who's who and where they are.

Professional associations will connect you with people in specific industries or professions. Check out the business calendar in your local paper and find out what associations are meeting when, and where. Then show up. This is a great place to make connections. Ask how you can get involved. Volunteer. Be visible.

There are probably non-profit services or social issues important to you. Learn more about them, including who sits on their boards of directors. If you see a name of someone from your industry, profession, or targeted company, make a note. You have a new connection with this person—something in common. This little piece of information could be the ice-breaker that gets you introduced later on.

You probably know this, but it's worth the reminder. Always be very respectful of how you make your connections. A direct mail campaign asking for a finance job, sent to the board of your local Habitat for Humanity organization because you volunteered with them once, is not the way to go. Be strategic and professional. Identify who you'd like to make a connection with and then use your personal networks for help. You usually get only one opportunity to get in front of the power players in your business community. Use the opportunity wisely.

Social media sites such as LinkedIn are also good resources for contact research. Find out who is working at your target companies or in your profession. Then work through your contacts to see if anyone can make an introduction for you.

Taking the time to learn more about your industry, targeted companies, and potential contacts will help you appear smarter, better informed, and better prepared than most job seekers. Set yourself apart from the other candidates.

Do your homework. Research, research, research.

Chapter 7

Take Center Stage and Perform Exceptionally

Ace Your Interview

You've dreamed about it. You're the understudy watching from the wings, waiting for your chance to take the stage and show them what you've got. You know you can play the part. Then it happens. The lead starlet does what everyone was telling her to do. She breaks a leg. And now it's your chance. Same play, different cast. You've been invited for an interview. You've been given the opportunity. This is your chance to shine. You're prepared. You're confident. You are the star of this event. *Take center stage and perform exceptionally.*

You are the Expert

What is it about an interview that turns your stomach like The Wild Thing ride at the fair? Hmmm… could it be that it requires you to talk about and sell yourself? Or that you have to think on your feet as someone asks what you consider to be really stupid questions? Or is it that you just aren't sure you're good enough for the job?

Whatever the reason for your anxiety, it is possible to get your stomach and nerves under control. The interview could feel more like a bumper car ride—not too scary, but it shakes you up a little bit with no permanent damage.

Here's the scoop on the interview. It is simply a conversation. They ask you questions, and you give them information. You ask them questions, and they give you information. Unfortunately, you probably get overly concerned about what questions they're going to ask. And that's what causes the butterflies to start fluttering way too fast, gives you that cotton mouth experience, and kicks your sweat glands into working overtime. You're afraid you won't know the answers. But think about that for a moment. They're asking you questions about *you*. Nobody knows you better than you do! It's not like a math test where there is only one right answer. You just need to know *you*—your skills, experience, and interests—and how they fit with the position you're applying for.

Before you go for your interview, think about your work experience and skills. Remind yourself of the ways you've added value to your former department or company. Take a walk down memory lane and remember your amazing accomplishments. You have a lot to offer your next employer.

Know yourself. Be yourself.

Behavioral-Based Interviewing

The best predictor of future performance is past performance. So employers will want to know what you've done in the past—how you made decisions, how you addressed issues, how you responded to different situations. Their best tool to get this information? The behavioral-based interview.

In a behavioral-based interview, the interviewer gathers and evaluates your past work experiences. The interviewer has (or should have) identified the knowledge, skills, and abilities critical to success on the job. These competencies lay the foundation for the questions that need to be asked. These questions will be open-ended (requiring more than a yes or no answer), and create an opportunity for you to describe examples of how you have responded to different situations in the past. Then it's up to the interviewer to evaluate whether or not you can demonstrate those key behaviors on their job.

Most behavioral-based interview questions will begin with "Tell me about a time…Describe a situation…Give me an example of…Think of an occasion when you…" Your challenge is to tell/describe/give/think of examples that show them you've got what they're looking for.

The best way to prepare for this type of interview is to identify successful work experiences that showcase your skills, prove you're a hard worker, and demonstrate that people enjoy working with you. I call these examples "stories." If you can clearly and succinctly articulate five or six stories, you will find it quite easy to sell yourself (which is the point of the interview).

Here's an example. In response to the question, "Tell me how you handle conflict on the job," Mary might answer like this: "Well, Ms. Interviewer, if I'm having trouble with someone at work, I think it's important we talk about it. We need to figure out how to keep things from blowing out of proportion." Did Mary's response tell you anything about how she's handled conflict in the past? No. Did her response tell you whether or not she is good at handling conflict? No.

Here's a better response to that same question. "Well, Ms. Interviewer, if I'm having trouble with someone at work, I think it's important we talk about it. We need to figure out how to keep things from blowing out of proportion. For example, last month a co-worker and I couldn't agree on a billing procedure. He wanted to hold all bills until the end of the day and then get them processed at the same time. I preferred to get the bills processed as they came in throughout the day. I suggested we sit down and talk about the pros and cons of each method. We did that, and came up with a compromise—we'd hold bills until noon and then process them throughout the afternoon. I'm glad we talked about the issue. I didn't realize it was taking me more time to stop doing my other work every time a bill came in."

Mary demonstrated how she's dealt with conflict in the past. Her response gives Ms. Interviewer a good idea of how she'll handle it in the future.

Creating Your Stories.

Your stories are clear, short, and focused. Here's your format: Problem, Action, Result (PAR).

Describe the **problem** very briefly. ("A co-worker and I couldn't agree on the billing procedure.") Then describe the **action** you took to address the problem. ("I suggested we sit down and talk about the pros and cons of each method.") Then describe the **result**. ("We did that, and came up with a compromise—we'd hold bills until noon and then process them throughout the afternoon.") Discuss the situation in the first person—tell the story with you in it.

A common mistake is to spend too much time detailing the problem. Remember, the interviewer is going to be most interested in the *action* you took.

Move quickly from the problem into what you did to makes things better, easier, faster, etc.

> "I was interviewing for an HR position in a professional services organization. I wanted this job really bad. I spent a fair amount of time thinking about my past jobs and what I'd accomplished at each, preparing for questions I anticipated they'd ask. They used behavioral-based interview techniques and I felt good that I had at least one situation to use in response to each question. I left thinking I'd nailed the interview!
>
> "The hiring manager was willing to give me frank feedback when he called a few days later to tell me I wasn't selected for the job. He felt that my experience (as I'd so thoroughly described) demonstrated skill in transactional work more than it demonstrated skills in what they were seeking. What's funny is I felt like I possessed the skills they were seeking. But when I selected my stories, I failed to describe those skills. I talked too much about what I'd done in my current position, regardless of its relevance to their position. I didn't describe how my experience translated into what I could do for them."
>
> ~ Cindy G.

Here's the neat thing about having several stories in your toolbox to use as examples of your success. You can use them to respond to different questions.

The conflict example I used could also be used to answer the question, "Tell me about a time when you had a disagreement with a co-worker." Or, "Tell me about a time when you changed a procedure at work." But remember, don't use the same story over and over again in the same interview. Pull together different stories that highlight different competencies and accomplishments. Make them relevant to the position you're applying for. Then practice telling them.

Before the Interview

Prepare. Prepare. Prepare.

Think about the questions you might be asked. What would you want to know if you were responsible for hiring for this position? What examples or stories best demonstrate your ability to do the job? Practice your answers.

My friend and colleague Cindy Greenwood is a seasoned HR professional. During her search for a new position, she knew she would be asked interview questions about competencies such as conflict resolution and problem solving. She knew she also had to demonstrate her functional expertise in benefits, employee relations, compensation, etc. So Cindy created a worksheet that listed the competencies and functions as headings. Then she thought back through her work history to recall achievements and situations she could use to respond to questions in those areas and noted them on her worksheet. It saved her the discomfort of blanking out and struggling through silence during the interview. She felt more prepared, and it showed.

Do your research. What's going on at the company? Changes? New products? Restructuring?

Know where your interview is scheduled and how you're going to get there. Any detours? Do you need change for parking meters? Do you have the correct name of the person you're meeting with?

During the Interview

No matter who you're interviewing with or for what job, several common courtesies are always appropriate:

- Give a firm handshake,
- Make eye contact,
- Arrive ten minutes early,
- Focus on the interviewer (remember, this is all about *their* needs, not yours),
- Show them you've done your homework,
- Make the connection between their needs and your experience.

One of the biggest mistakes people make in an interview is to talk about their job titles instead of their accomplishments. Does telling your potential employer you were a project analyst sell you? No. It only gives them a fact without demonstrated success. Instead, tell the interviewer *how* your work made a difference in your department and your company. I consistently tell my workshop participants to ask, "So what?" as they start listing their skills and responsibilities.

For example:

"I was a project analyst for three years."

So what?

"During my three years as a project analyst, I worked on two significant projects. One of them reduced our turnaround time by two months and the other saved our company about $3,000 annually. Which project would you like to hear more about?"

Good interviewers know you're going to be nervous. Listen to the questions and tell them what you've done. If you don't understand a question, ask for clarification. Show genuine interest in the position. Tell them you want the job. Remember to breathe.

After the Interview

This isn't the time to use gimmicks. First, it could make you look desperate, and second, it requires very keen intuition to know how the cutesy follow-up will be received. Most of us don't know enough about the interviewer after an hour to risk being too clever.

Many years ago an applicant sent me a shoe with a note tucked inside following our interview. He said he was so excited to "get one foot in the door." I'd give him an A for creativity, but what do I do with one shoe? A few years later a female applicant sent me a woman's long, white glove. She said she thought the position would "fit me like a glove." Now if I could only find a place where one shoe and one glove are appropriate attire...

The best follow-up to an interview is a sincere thank-you note, one that is handwritten and sent in an envelope with a stamp on it. (Yes, mail is still exchanged that way.) You can buy blank note cards in almost any store. Send the note that same or next day. Include three key messages in your note: 1) You appreciate the interviewer's time and you are very interested in the position. 2) You have what the company is looking for. Refer to a specific conversation or topic discussed during the interview. Make the connection between that discussion and your skills/experience. 3) You look forward to continued conversations about the position, and then reiterate your interest.

It's a good idea to wait about a week before following up with a phone call. Keep in mind that other candidates were probably interviewed, and filling this position isn't the only responsibility the interviewer has on his plate. Your follow-up phone call should be short and to the point. Key messages: 1) You are still very interested in the position and would like to move forward in the process. 2) Is there any other information you can provide while they're making their decision? 3) When can you expect to hear from them again? If you get the interviewer's voice mail, leave a message using the same, brief format.

Phone Interviews

The phone interview is typically used as a screening tool. The company usually wants to know three things:

1) What is your level of interest in the position?
2) Do you meet our minimum requirements (technical skills in particular)?
3) How good are your communication skills (listening, speaking, articulating, etc.)?

It is a really good thing if you get a phone interview. It means your resume caught their attention and/or someone has made a networking connection for you. Now the potential employer wants to know more about you.

The biggest challenge of a phone interview is the absence of a visual connection. You can't see them, and they can't see you. So your voice has to project your enthusiasm, focus, and sincerity without the support of your body language.

To set yourself up for success on a phone interview, I suggest three things:

1) Smile. It may feel corny if you're standing in the middle of your kitchen wearing sweatpants, but it works. Smiling brightens your tone and helps you sound more energetic.

2) Stand. If you sit during this interview, you're going to lose energy quickly. Standing keeps you focused and alert. Make sure, though, that your standing doesn't turn into pacing. It's easy to start moving when you're excited or nervous. Stand and plant yourself.

3) Use your "Success Notes." This is a 4 x 6 lined note card you've got in your job search file that highlights the four or five key points you want to make about this position. Remember, you are selling yourself. Be very clear on making the connection between what they need and what you have to offer. Your Success Notes reminds you of these points. I cover this a little more in chapter 9.

Because you can't see the person you're speaking with, your listening skills need to be working overtime. Listen for signals that indicate you're talking too much, or the interviewer has lost interest. Your best bet is to speak succinctly, and ask if she wants you to discuss the topic in more detail.

What Doesn't Work

There are several behaviors that are best left at home when interviewing face-to-face:
- Chewing gum
- Smelling like cigarette smoke (breath and/or clothing)

- Perfume or cologne (be aware of sensitivities)
- Arriving an hour early (seems too needy and puts pressure on the interviewer)
- Suggesting you should be hired because of your financial situation (not their problem)
- Walking in with a chip on your shoulder (vent before you interview).

The interview is your opportunity to tell your potential employer that you've got what it takes to do the job. Use your research. Use your stories. Use your experience.

**Know yourself. Be yourself.
Perform exceptionally.**

Chapter 8

Watch Miss America or Mr. Universe Pageants

Create a Strategy for Finding Your Next Job

The gowns. The muscles. The interviews. The poses. Pageant participants come to their events ready to win. Your job search deserves nothing less. Prepare for your job search as though your career depends on it. Develop your list of target companies. Create your list of networks. Perfect that resume. Practice interviewing. *Plan your work and then work your plan. Be prepared.*

It Doesn't Just Happen Overnight

As little girls, my sisters and I loved watching the Miss America pageant. We'd pick out the gowns we wanted to wear, use our homemade score cards to judge the talent competitions and cry when Bert Parks would sing, "There she is, Miss America." (If you don't remember Bert Parks, my apologies.) It all looked so easy. It still does.

What we don't see during that two-hour television show is the incredible amount of preparation and planning that takes place before the competition. A young woman doesn't wake up one day and decide she'll just show up that evening at the convention center and make a run for the crown. No, she puts together a long-term plan for competing and winning. It usually involves diet and exercise, speech coaches, modeling lessons, talent preparation, and practice, practice, practice.

Your job search requires that same type of planning and discipline. How do you do that?

1. Create your plan.
2. Work your plan.

We've talked about the importance of research, creating a resume that captures attention, following up on job leads, networking, interviewing, staying current, and taking care of yourself. Your Weekly Plan for Success pulls together all these components of a successful job search and helps you create and manage your time while focusing on the most important activities.

Your Weekly Plan for Success

I suggest that every Friday evening you take some time to identify the activities you need to focus on during the next week. Then pull out your calendar and schedule your week and your work. Plug in activities from these four categories:

- **Focus on Job Opportunities**—The action steps that get you closer to an interview and job.
- **Professional Development**—Activities that will improve your skills and marketability.
- **Networking**—Talking to individuals who can help you connect to opportunities or people.
- **Personal Support**—Scheduling time to do things that are fun and interesting.

Don't forget to check your local newspapers for association meetings, networking groups, lectures, or workshops you'll want to schedule and attend. If Johnny has a softball game Tuesday afternoon, you have the freedom to schedule around his game. Attend and enjoy the game, knowing you've got time scheduled for your job search work.

Here are a few examples of activities in each of these areas:

Focus on Job Opportunities
- Send out a resume and cover letter,
- Follow-up on a resume,
- Send a thank-you note to an interviewer,

- Research a company you're interested in,
- Attend a workshop for job seekers,
- Practice interviewing with someone who has interviewing experience.

Professional Development
- Take a computer class,
- Read a book or magazine article related to your professional field,
- Listen to a lecture or podcast related to your industry or field.

Networking
- Prepare your list of one hundred contacts or add to it,
- Call three people on your networking list and identify follow-up action steps,
- Contact someone in your field or industry for an informational interview,
- Attend a professional association meeting.

Personal Support
- Exercise, move, walk,
- Volunteer,
- Invite another job seeker to coffee and make it all about them,
- Take time for solitude, meditation, or reflection. Be grateful. Breathe.

> "What I wish I would have done earlier in my search: I would have more quickly enrolled in some continuing education or other courses as a way of exploring other career options. But I kept thinking that by the time I picked one, got funding, and got registered I would be employed. I should have just jumped into some classes."
>
> ~ John H.

You will find a Weekly Plan for Success worksheet at **http://www.SignificantSolutionsInc.com/BigSuccess.html.** I've also included an example there of a completed worksheet so you can see how it works. You will find this to be one of the most important tools you use during your search. You just need to add the discipline and follow-through.

**Plan your work. Work your Plan.
Be prepared.**

Chapter 9

Develop a Simple System for Big Success

Organize Your Job Search Materials

Sammie's side of our phone conversation sounded something like this. "Hello? Yeah, this is Sammie. Oh, hi. What job did you say this is about? Hmm… I'm sorry…can you remind me about the position? I don't remember which one this is. Oh, sorry. I don't have my stuff in front of me. Why do I want the job? I've been looking for about two months and this sounds like something that would be interesting."

So tell me. What would be the level of your interest in talking more to Sammie about the position? Mine was pretty low. You never know when your shot at a position is coming. Be prepared. *Set up a system that will help you sound like the professional you are.*

Setting Up Your Simple System

Your system is simply this:

- In a designated area, you have the resources you need to connect with your network and potential employers.
- In this same area, you have a place to efficiently file your job search material.

You may love this chapter. The thought and anticipation of setting up a work area and a job search system raises your pulse and gives you the goose bumps. You could spend hours in your local office products store. So many organizing gadgets, so little time. You can't wait to get started.

Or you may want to quickly skip over this chapter. Your pulse is racing and you've got the goose bumps, but it's because you know you can't organize your way out of a paper bag. You walk into an office product store and just stare at the rows of stuff. What on earth do people do with all this stuff?

So here's the deal. *You* will decide how elaborate and colorful and detailed your Simple System is. The important point is that you have a system. Its purpose? To make your life easier. I guarantee that having your job search material organized—in a way that works for you—will save you hours of frustration and embarrassment.

A couple suggestions as you create your work area and system. Find a place other than the kitchen table. You want your work area to be your designated workspace. It's a space that makes it easy for you to get to your computer, phone, files, and other job search material and supplies. You don't want to be moving everything from the table to the counter to the dresser and back to the table. And set yourself up in a quiet area. Make it easy to stay focused. When those phone conversations and interviews start, you don't want to worry about the background chatter.

Your system shouldn't require a how-to manual for using it. Keep it simple. The most important and basic component: a file folder for each position you've applied for. Place any material you have on a position into its corresponding file folder. Then put these files in a box by your card table or desk. And if you're one of those who loves the idea of designing and managing your own office? Use your own creativity to create a space that inspires and motivates you. Use different colored files and organizing racks to distinguish different categories. Buy a notebook with an interesting design—something that gets your creative juices going. Make it your own.

An important reminder for every job seeker: job search expenses (i.e., resume expenses, travel, telephone, seminar fees, etc.) are often deductible. Save your receipts and track your expenses. Start a file called Job Search Expenses. When you're preparing your taxes, make sure you discuss how much of your expenses are eligible for a tax break with an accountant or tax advisor.

The Simple System for Big Success

What you need:
- ☐ Table or desk
- ☐ File folders
- ☐ Phone
- ☐ Computer (or know where to access one)
- ☐ Typing paper
- ☐ Notebook (ideally, one you can carry with you)
- ☐ Address book (electronic or hard copy)
- ☐ Business cards (don't worry about a title—your contact information is most important)
- ☐ Pens
- ☐ Calendar
- ☐ 4 x 6 lined note cards
- ☐ Thank-you note cards (blank inside)
- ☐ Stamps
- ☐ A 3-ring binder that will store your Weekly Plan for Success worksheets, your networking sheets discussed in chapter 5 (if you aren't tracking them electronically), and other job search material

Setting Up Your System

1. Create a new file for every job you apply for. Keep it filed on your desk. On the file tab write the company name and position you're applying for. (We Make Widgets, Inc.—Financial Analyst)

2. Create an electronic file on your computer that's called My Job Search. Within this folder you will create a folder for each job you apply for.

3. Include in the position file (electronic and/or hard copy):

   - a copy of the posting or ad,
   - a copy of your resume and cover letter,
   - a log of all contacts with the company,
   - your Success Notes for this specific position (described later).

4. Create folders with relevant material to your job search: networking, associations, job search tips, etc. You can decide if you prefer to file them electronically or as hard copy. Keep it simple.

I've suggested you set up both an electronic file and a desk file for positions you've applied for. Why? A desk file will be easy to grab if a potential employer calls and you can take it with you. Since so much of your job search work is done electronically, computer files make good sense. Don't make your system more complicated than it needs to be. If you prefer to use only one system, then set it up that way. Choose a system that works for you.

If you'd rather have a root canal than set up an organized system, at least try and create a file folder for each job you apply for. Know where your information is.

Your Success Notes

Your Success Notes are written on a 4 x 6 lined note card. They highlight why you are the best fit for the position you're applying for. Here's out it works. As soon as you apply for a position, identify the four or five key points that connect your experience with what that employer is specifically looking for. Every time you communicate with someone from that company, you will make sure you hit on these key points (i.e., during the phone interview, in your cover letter, at your interview). When you're called for a quick phone interview, you simply pull out your file on the position they're calling about, and you've got your main talking points—your Success Notes—right in front of you. When you're applying for a lot of positions, this will save you time and keep you focused on what's most important to the caller.

Advice From the Pro

Audrey Thomas is a friend, colleague, and owner of Organized Audrey. (I bet you can guess what her business does.) I have referred her to family, friends, and clients. She knows her stuff and has the reputation to prove it. Here are a few of her organizing suggestions for job seekers.

Develop a Simple System for Big Success

"You need to have a system in place for organizing the information and material you collect and distribute during your job search. The last thing you need is to lose or misplace the name and phone number of someone you were supposed to follow up with regarding a future job. For information contained on paper, create file folders with categories such as Prospective Employers, Portfolio Items, and Research. Just like a filing cabinet, your computer hard drive is important in organizing electronic information you receive/send during a job search. Keep any notes, feedback, or comments in your folders along with business cards and other information you gather during the hiring process.

"Because so much of our information today is sent via email, be sure to take advantage of your email management system by setting up file folders to hold important email notifications/communication related to your job search. Equally important, have a reliable calendar that will help you with appointment times and deadlines. You might prefer a paper calendar/planner or an electronic version like Outlook. Either way, find a calendar system that you can depend on to get you where you need to be in order to find that next job."

~ Audrey Thomas

You are going to create and gather a lot of material and information during your job search. Make it easy on yourself. Put your material in a place where you can quickly find it.

Set up a simple system that will help you appear as the professional you are.

Chapter 10

Keep Your Eye on the Ball

Stay Focused on Finding a Job

*W*hen it comes to sports, there's nothing more important than keeping your eye on the ball, or the basket, or the end zone. You get the picture. The same is true when you're looking for a job. You must stay focused on your number one goal—finding a job. It is easy to get distracted and disappointed—discouraging rejection letters, projects at home that have your name written all over them. It seems so necessary to take the day off, or the week, or the month. Don't give in. Your job search is too important. Create a balance of work, play, and networking, but never take your eye off the ball. *Focus. Find a job.*

You've Gotta' Play the Game to Win the Game

It is so easy to get distracted. Projects you've been wanting to finish for years are screaming your name. "Finish me now! You'll never have another break like this! Choose me! Choose me!" This seems like the perfect time to clean the garage, build the patio, get the kids' scrapbooks done, and paint the living room. Are you sure about that? Yes, unemployment results in hours that aren't scheduled—seemingly more free time. And yes, this could be a time to get some projects done around the house. But remember: the only way you will find your next job is if you work at it. You won't find a job putting up sheetrock in the basement.

Tell those little voices you will respond to their urgent requests, *and* their requests are secondary to finding a job. It's great if you want to work on projects, but schedule them around your job search activities. Your number one priority is to find a job.

You've probably watched a reality TV show. The contestants spend every waking hour building alliances to win the prize (networking), strategizing how to win the prize (creating their plans), and competing for the prize (working their plans). Their single-minded focus and intensity are amazing. You will need a very similar focus. You are fortunate that, unlike the reality TV contestants, you don't need to be playing the game twenty-four hours a day, seven days a week.

Determine how many hours each day you want to put into your job search. Then identify how you're going to spend those hours—the activities you're going to do that will get you closer to getting hired. When you were employed by someone else, you had working hours you needed to commit to, expectations that needed to be met, and duties that needed to be completed. Create the same structure for your job search.

Keeping your focus also allows you to enjoy the time you're not working on your job search. You know you have hours scheduled to network, research, write, call, and follow-up. So you can give yourself permission to relax or spend time working on projects without feeling guilty. Once you've made your calendar commitments, schedule in the projects, extra time with family, or activities that refresh and rejuvenate you.

Find a balance of work and play. Use your Weekly Plan for Success to help you stay on track.

Keep your eye on the ball.
Focus.

Chapter 11

Go Fishin'

Take Time for Yourself

You will experience highs and lows during this career transition. It's part of the process. You don't know if your transition will last a month or a year. Focusing only on your job search will make you crazy and drive those around you nuts. Make sure you give yourself a break sometimes, emotionally and physically. *You need to rejuvenate and re-energize yourself.* Give yourself a treat. Read a good book, sit in the sun, or go to an afternoon matinee. Take care of yourself. Go fishin'.

It's about Balance

Mark had always been a star at We Make Widgets, Inc. His performance reviews were great, he'd moved up the ladder quickly, and people genuinely enjoyed working with him. So he was shocked when he was told his position had been eliminated. His first plan of action? Get the message out to everybody that he was looking for another job. He spent the first thirty days of being unemployed feverishly trying to find work. He worked ten hours a day mass mailing his resume, searching websites, responding to ads, calling friends and former colleagues, and asking almost everyone he met if they were hiring. He didn't dare leave his computer for fear he'd miss an email or an updated job site. And on Day 31? He collapsed. He was physically and emotionally drained. He spent the next month wondering what to do next.

Jane was also known as a high potential, high performer employee at We Make Widgets, Inc. When her job was eliminated she felt betrayed, embarrassed, and numb. She spent the first couple days sitting in her apartment and walking the dog. Then she decided to apply the skills that had made her successful at We Make Widgets to her job search.

Jane sat down and created a plan of action. She identified one hundred people who could help her move closer to her goal of getting a job. She scheduled the job search activities she would commit to each week. She'd always wanted to take a Pilates class, so she signed up for one at the local YMCA. (She hadn't entered those doors for two years—it felt good to be taking some time to get back in shape.) She had always dreamed of putting together scrapbooks for her two nieces. On her calendar, she scheduled three times each week when she'd work on them. For those first thirty days, she worked her plan and followed her schedule. And on Day 31? She had more energy and more focus. She had made several exceptional networking contacts and lined up two informational interviews. Her down times were not as frequent and they were replaced with the pride she had in her disciplined approach. The time spent on her nieces was reminding her of the good things in her life. And the icing on the cake—she'd had lost a few inches.

The difference between Mark and Jane's approaches to their job searches is clear. Mark got caught up in needing to do something—right away—very intensely. He went into panic mode and stayed there too long. Jane knew she had to find a balance between finding a job and taking care of herself. She knew it could be months before she found a new job, and she needed to pace herself.

Who do you think will feel better three months down the road? Who do you think will be ready to start a new job, hitting the ground running, when the opportunity comes along?

It is difficult to think of your job search as a full-time job, especially in the early days and weeks. So much energy is used in just processing and dealing with the fact that you've lost your job. You need more time than usual to think, meditate, pray, and plan.

My suggestion? Consider putting in twenty-five to thirty hours each week on your job search. Use these hours to network, research, attend workshops, study, apply for jobs, and follow-up. Use the rest of the time to take care of yourself emotionally and physically. Do the things that bring you joy and refresh your spirit. Your Weekly Plan for Success is a critical tool in helping you create the balance you need. Schedule your most important job search activities on your calendar first. Then schedule the fun things you want to do that will energize you.

The success of your job search depends on your daily, individual choices. At the end of the day put all your choices together. You end up with either a day of productive work and an energized spirit, or a day of lost opportunities and increased anxiety. It's your choice.

Keep your life balanced.
Go fishin'.

Significance and Success!

A Note From Gaye

During the early days in my career, I wished for and worked in challenging positions, fast movement up the corporate ladder, and the salary and perks that go along with the right titles. Nothing wrong with working for and wanting those things. I have had, and continue to have, amazing opportunities to work with some very bright and interesting people. Each job, each boss, and each co-worker has been a gift, helping me become the person I am today, preparing me for the person I want to become.

During the last few years I started to wonder how those great positions, perks, and titles fit into the bigger picture of my life. I spent a lot of time thinking about why I'm on this earth and what I'm called to do. I believe that I have been created by an Almighty God who has a plan for me. I'm not here by accident. He has given me talents, resources, and opportunities to serve others. He has also seen me through the missteps, bad decisions, and mistakes that helped me grow.

This introspection and reflection have helped me discover what gives me the greatest energy and fulfillment. As a result, my professional priorities have changed. Now I focus on interesting projects with clients that engage and challenge me. The ideal perks are flexibility to spend time with family and work that takes me to interesting places. My work hours are many (sometimes too many), but they no longer define the rest of my life. Writing and speaking opportunities have appeared as I have made room for them.

Looking back, I realize it was so easy to blame my schedule for the stress in my life. Ooftah! (That's a Norwegian word I use when I'm amazed or surprised by something. I use it quite frequently.) What I neglected to acknowledge was the schedule only shows what I put on it. It doesn't control me—I control it. My calendar is a reflection of my priorities, combined with my Midwestern work ethic. Midwestern folks just plain work hard.

So what has this to do with finding a job? Plenty.

As frustrating as unemployment is, see the gift in it. This is time to spend contemplating, discovering, and creating the life you want to live. What do you want to do? Who do you want to be? What legacy do you want to leave? What's really important to you? What does success look and feel like for you?

Significance and Success are sometimes seen as being mutually exclusive. Some might say significance follows success in some hierarchy of making a difference. Perhaps that's true. But I like to believe we can be significant *and* successful. I am significant because no one else can be me. I consider myself successful when I am doing the work I love, in a way that brings me joy, while contributing to the goals of those whom I serve.

Your transition journey is an important part of your life. You have skills and abilities the world needs. I am hopeful you will find the right place to use those gifts. My prayer is that in your journey you will discover your definition of success, and embrace the fact that **you are significant**.

Please let me know how I can help you discover or re-discover your significance, your purpose, your definition of success. I'd love to hear from you.

Gaye Lindfors
Gaye@SignificantSolutionsInc.com

Resources

Bureau of Labor's Occupational Outlook
www.bls.gov/oco

For hundreds of different types of jobs, the Occupational Outlook Handbook tells you the training and education needed, earnings, expected job prospects, what workers do on the job, and working conditions. The site also links you to job market information for each state.

Unemployment Benefits
www.unemployment-resources.org/states

The Unemployment Insurance Program provides temporary benefits to qualified persons out of work through no fault of their own. The purpose of the program is to help maintain the economic stability within a community. The UI fund is financed entirely by a special tax paid by employers.

Workforce Investment Act – Adults and
Dislocated Workers Program
www.doleta.gov/programs/general_info.cfm

Provides quality and employment training services. Provides a link to state services.

Forms You Can Download

To access the forms and samples that will help you get started on your job search, go to **http://www.SignificantSolutionsInc.com/BigSuccess.html.**

- Resume sample
- Tracking My Accomplishments
- My Weekly Plan for Success

About the Illustrator

Sue Heinemann has illustrated and designed greeting cards, worked twelve years as a graphic designer, and is a professional photographer. She specializes in photographing weddings, portraits and illustrative photography. Her photography achievements are many, including Loan Awards from the Professional Photographers of America, the Kodak Commercial Gallery Award displayed at Epcot, and the Fuji Masterpiece Award. Sue also won the MN Professional Illustrative Photographer of the Year Award.

Sue gets her best ideas when she runs. She has completed forty-eight marathons.

Sue lives in Chanhassen, MN. You can reach her at **smhein@aol.com**.

About the Author

Gaye Lindfors is a small business advisor, speaker, and author. She has worked with hundreds of individuals who want to make the connection between intentional living and meaningful work. Prior to starting her own company, Significant Solutions, Inc., she was responsible for the hiring of thousands of employees in Fortune 500 companies and non-profit organizations. She knows what employers are looking for and understands the heart of the job seeker.

Her organizational development expertise and experience have helped business owners transform the way they do business. She specializes in making the connection between employees who want to bring their best to work and employers who want to bring out the best in their employees.

As a national speaker, Gaye is known for her ability to generate enthusiasm, engage the hearts and minds of her audience, and focus people on living and working with purpose. She is a contributing author to the book, *Don't Miss Your Boat: Living Your Life with Purpose in the Real World.* Gaye has her M.A. in Industrial Relations and is a member of the National Speakers Association (NSA). She and her husband, Steve, live in St. Paul, MN.

Contact Gaye at:
Gaye@SignificantSolutionsInc.com.

For more information visit:
www.SignificantSolutionsInc.com.